Worm Food and Bone Sand

poems by
Caitlin Ellis

Worm Food and Bone Sand
©Caitlin Ellis, 2022

All Rights Reserved.

The author supports copyright as we believe this fuels creativity and promotes free speech.

Thank you for complying with the copyright laws by not reproducing, scanning, or distributing any part of it in any form without permission, except for the purpose of review and promotion of the work.

Poetry by Caitlin Ellis

Design and edited by
Rebecca Rijsdijk
rebeccarijsdijk.com

Cover image by Jan van Kessel the elder.
Author photo by Shaina Bostin
Illustration by Emma Vagg

Thanks for reading.

for the growing
and the grown

"And so, being young and dipt in folly
I fell in love with melancholy."

— Edgar Allan Poe

Contents

Foreword

Cobwebs	13
The Burning Glass	14
Little Thorns in the Back of the Throat	16
Growing Pains	17
Cabin Fever	18
Regret	19
I'm Worried About Her	20
Desensitised	21
Submerged	22
Shame	23
Embers	24
Not Sober	25
Not Yet	26
Parasites	27
Summer's Funeral	28
Duality	29
Naked	30

Mine	31
Weeds Between Pavers	32
Rising Tides	34
New Love	35
Growth in Decay	36
A Clouded Mind	38
Sunset	39
Sweet Promises	40
We Are the Madmen	41
Teenage Vulnerability	42
Like Rain	43
The Right Words	44
Traces of Rubble	45
Gifts from the Tree of Knowledge	46
Worm Food, Bone Sand	47
The Becoming	48

Acknowledgements
About the Author

CW: mental illness, substance use, sexual trauma
Please take care as you read.

Dear Reader,

There is something terrifying about sharing your work with the world. If you're creative in any way, you know this to be true. This collection feels like a time capsule to me; a small and quiet burial of moments and feelings from my teens left for me to return to in the years to come.

Worm Food and Bone Sand is bittersweet. Equal parts heartbreaking and heart-warming. It is also far from perfect. I could re-write these poems till the end of time, but what good would that do? The Caitlin who wrote these (in all her awkward teenage glory) has grown, but these poems remain as they are: placeholders in time.

I hope as you read, you are reminded of what it meant to be young and confused and wonderfully naïve. I hope it reminds you of the constellation of "firsts" you experience in your teenage years and makes you feel held and remembered.

My heart is in your hands.

All my love,
Caitlin xx

Cobwebs

Line, line, number nine,
spider crawling up my spine,
laggard legs and idle touch,
tingling from its silent clutch,
over limbs and under clothes
(keep my eyes and mouth shut closed)
heart kicked into fight or flight
(you never know when it may bite)
squish it, swipe it, flick away –
still, its cobwebs tend to stay.

The Burning Glass

We sit around a chipped old brick,
a crew of fiends in summer's sun,
curiosity gripped by boredom,
a shard of glass held in angelic fun.

I, a head shorter than the others,
sit high on the back of my heels to see
the tallest raise his glittering sedition
to the yellow warmth of afternoon glee.

He flips a heavy brick, betraying
small round balls of drowsy delusion.
The slaters, now victims of our foolish wrath,
unfold in a hurry to escape the intrusion,

but he is quicker than their hurried rush
and he catches the light with the glass,
while I watch in ashen realisation as
a pinprick beam burns through the grass.

He laughs a devilish laugh

and sees the horror on my face,
he hands to me the shard of glass
and says that I must take his place.

So, I take from him the burning glass,
smudged and dirtied by our fingers,
then let it catch the fiery sky
and burn the poor fools that linger.

Little Thorns in the Back of the Throat are the Hardest to Remove

It's a tickle at first.
A small little thorn.
Easy pickings for trained tweezers –
just a little tug at that well known
little-but-not-so-little
(actually reasonably large),
pink and white flurry of
hot flashes and cold shakes
and steadily building nausea
in my stomach, throat, face, eyes –

and it dawns on me
that I have, once again, fallen
for my own self-defeating tricks
as I press the thorn back into
 its fleshy hole.

Worm Food and Bone Sand

GROWING PAINS

Belly cramps
aching bones
splitting skin
piercing groans

                                     Crooked guts
                                   wicked-spined
                                   mangled limbs
                                   all intertwined

Lurid lungs
venom breath
glutinous brain
awaiting death

                                High-strung tendons
                                     famished heart
                                       all this pain
                                   is just the start.

CABIN FEVER

I crave fresh air like my demons crave isolation:
tongue dripping at the thought,
eyes weeping at the idea,
mind spiralling into a perverse frenzy.

Back arched.
Teeth bared.
Ears pricked.

Woman or monster?
I am a slave to my own obsessions.

REGRET

You cling to me like a leech:
cold, famished, desperate.
You dig your teeth into my flesh,
break the skin,
and suck me dry.

I'M WORRIED ABOUT HER

The last time we caught eyes,
I swear I saw a ghost; her hollow eyes
ran a dull chill up my crooked spine,
and gulped the scream straight from
my gaping mouth. She was starved,
and I was empty, and we both
stared longingly into what we knew were
empty platters licked clean of crumbs.

I'm worried about her,
        and by that I mean

I'm worried about what she could do,
        and by that I mean

I'm worried about me.

DESENSITISED

Empty, except for:

cold
sliding doors
them, adjacent

tight throat
linen
and
and

empty, except for:

cold
sliding doors
them, adjacent
and
and

SUBMERGED

I often forget that I am a creature of air
until I dive head-first into the deep blue.

My lungs long for liberation,
to be released from the liquid prison
I so love to submerge them in.

We fight, my lungs and I, as I strive to
dig deeper into the distant depths of the sea
and sink my sinner soul so that it may
decorate the ocean floor like a carcass
left for feasting.

Alas, my lungs protest,
pulling damned soul and starved body
back to salty, stinking surface.

SHAME

Loving something disgusting
is like a double-edged sword:
one edge cuts my heart,
the other cuts my tongue.

Blood runs from self-inflicted wounds
blue and choked, coagulating
between teeth and gum.

I chew on clots like
raspberry gummies and
pray the stains in my teeth
remain silent behind
pursed lips.

EMBERS

Hot embers fly,
caught in a tangle of smoke
and midnight breeze.
The flames dance in their prison,
but they dance, nonetheless.

The wood is in agony,
but it burns for the fire
to feel its warmth,
see its spark,
hear its hiss and crackle–
just one last time.

Somewhere, the moon sings.

Its silver face is melancholic,
but the lullaby is sweet.
It welcomes flying embers
into its cold embrace.

NOT SOBER

Let me feel the ceiling on my face,
the weight, a blanket for my mind.
Let me roll in blurs of bliss,
desolate as the bottle I just finished.
for me, myself, and I.
Because I like
downside up and outside in,
I like that sinking spiral–

spinning,

    spinning,

        spinning...

Let me sip ambrosia now and
cough up poison tomorrow.

NOT YET

What of the wave of nausea
that claws up my throat
and wells in my eyes?

I have tamed stranger beasts.
This one– a humble foreboding too timid
for elevated speech– is but a
precursor of harsher truths.

Perhaps it would be kinder on my bones;
death rattle will come,
but this is not it.

Still, I spend more time in my grave
than my bedroom,
and the life that flashes before me
feels real all the same.

This lucid foreign landscape
is not mine – at least not quite.
Not yet.

PARASITES

How is it that our traumas
can sit like parasites in our lungs,
shortening all our breaths
and holding back our tongues?

SUMMER'S FUNERAL

I am forever perplexed by routine,
the joyless, pitiful cycle of waking up new,
only to fall asleep old once more.

New is sly as the sun
that deserts me for months
only to taunt me behind cotton candy clouds
I can't even taste.

Next summer.

I have no patience for this rigmarole of
incessant, heedless, godforsaken
put-me-back-to-sleep existence.

No effort is too small,
And yet here I am– once more.

DUALITY

Two parts of a well-defined whole,
the shackle to an innocent hand,
grappling with a grief
forgiven only with suffering–
pinpricks to a cursed and cushioned heart,
a game of elite execration.

I need no cage greater than
the one I've built myself.

NAKED

Let's pretend that you can't see me
all muscle-tendon-bone,
that I don't glisten red
and dust off chalky beige
when you get down to it.

It's not quite so lovely
under this soft, cling-wrapped
surface and the dainty illusion of

Something B I G G E R.

It's a little *lonely*,
a little *plain*,
a little *boring*,
a little...*human underneath*,
when you truly get down to it.

MINE

Her mouth is pursed–
a diamond-encrusted zip,
and I cut my skin
as I kiss her lip.

WEEDS BETWEEN PAVERS

Tonight, my grief struck my heart,
my body quivered as my soul quaked,
and my sorrow overflowed through
the sinuses of yesterday's memories.

...past...present...future...

A reel-viewer toying with
every minute come to pass,
a mockery of mortality.

Mortality.

An old friend we've trained so well
to hide in our shadows, easily forgotten till
the hairs on the backs of our necks remind us
that *we too* are nothing.

This world did not make room for you and me.
We are as insignificant as weeds between pavers,
fillers for the mundane–

the world's latest trick.

Though I'll take this small miracle –
that I can smell life as well as I can smell decay –
and I will mourn each mouth-watering second
of this meaningless existence
till my teeth turn black.

RISING TIDES

My blood crashes against the cage of my heart–
a tide seeking cavernous walls to throw itself upon
again, and again, and again.

Listen closely and you'll hear
the songs of my hopes, my dreams,
my secrets and my aches–
beautifully melancholic.

I wait for an ear,
a soul whose blood runs like rain
off the sails of a long-lost vessel,
to bend over,
to press their head against my chest,
and listen to the murmurs of the ocean within me.

NEW LOVE

Messed sheets hold in their folds
secrets passed between soft lips,
whispered in shallow breaths,
and caught by cautious teeth.

GROWTH IN DECAY

My thoughts do venture backwards
for each *'now'* is but a *'then,'*

just crooked little fossils
all resurfacing again.

These forever ageing shells are just a
a semblance of the past;

each atom in our bodies
relics used and now recast.

Death is in our blood, good friend,
decay is in our bones,

my eyes (your eyes) my voice (your voice):
recycled cornerstones.

We come from nothing– you know that–
but I wish to make it clear:

I am death, behold me.

for it is by death

that we are here.

A CLOUDED MIND

In my mind, the rain fell like
a soft shower that never ceased.
Every drop touched a different part of
my soul and washed it clean.

Droplets ran down my cheeks,
carrying with them mud
as dark as the thoughts that
hung like a cloud above my head.

But the cloud had done its hanging
and it soothed my burning skin
with ice-cold drops of mercy.

SUNSET

She parted with the day frantically:
golden fingernails clawing at every
tree, roof tile and inch of tarmac–
a desperate charade of her love
for all things within reach.

Unwilling to give way to the darkness,
refusing to be stifled by biting cold,
her frenzied fiasco left a bitter trail of
blush and blue bruising in the solemn sky.

SWEET PROMISES

Your kisses are delicate moments
of pure bliss captured between
our lips.

I forget things in an instant,
my mind blank
and yet
full of you.

For a moment,
there is a heaven,
the sweet taste
of redemption,
freedom,
eternity on my tongue.
I never want our lips to part,
the dam you've built in my mind
to falter. You promise me
forever in a moment.

WE ARE THE MADMEN

The night flashed before us,
a black and white haze filled with colour,
a silence so loud our ears rang,
our feet hitting the ground so hard
it didn't hurt.

Hands held, clammily, tight.
Hearts shudder, race, drop.
Eyes dart, close, open.
Mouths smile, laugh, sing.

Crowing into the night like the madmen we are,
the moment melts like wax,
lost in an unforgettable breath.

TEENAGE VULNERABILITY

We trade body parts like
secret notes passed during class,
hands searching for the strange,
the new,
the oddly familiar.

I bare my vulnerability
in the hopes that losing the tooth
means gold coins under
the pillow next morning–

though I forget we're still
brushed tenderly with the awkward,
bashful innocence of youth,
so it is your own vulnerability
I find under my pillow–
still golden, still precious.

LIKE RAIN

Suddenly, I understood the rain:

how it fell,
why it fell.

I understood why first it sprinkled,
and then, without notice,
it poured.

The rain reminded me of you,
because the rain was falling
for the earth,
and I was falling for you,
and neither of us knew
when the storm would end.

THE RIGHT WORDS

I feel like there are words for everything,
yet no words for anything at all,

and I want to scream a thousand into the sky,
hurtling my bitterness and my passion
through a solar system beyond my reach.

I need to bleed out onto a page
until it is so covered in ink
it becomes drenched with my mind.

I want to breathe in all the right words
so, just this once, I can sigh
all the right ones back out.

TRACES OF RUBBLE

Soft like suede, but not quite–
rough around the edges,
half gnawed, small tears,
traces of rubble from
lost thoughts and daydreams,
cracks and valleys,
the worn and the new,
it all melts like fairy-floss
at the tip of your tongue.

GIFTS FROM THE TREE OF KNOWLEDGE

I'll take my hot, sweet tea,
my crisp linen and my picnic set,
my lazy summer afternoons laced
with apple cider and babbling company,
my late-night board games
and my quiet innocence.

But,
I will also take my drunken adventures,
my insatiable lust-driven cravings,
my blood-curdling anger and
my delicious, wicked passions.

I'll take the wine with the holy water
and the flames over the ground.

God couldn't give us heaven
without a taste of hell.

WORM FOOD, BONE SAND

From dust, I come, and to dust, I'll return.
Worm food and bone sand,
I'll infiltrate the earth as it infiltrates me.

It is I who will roar in the sandstorms
and hiss salty foam as the waves hit the shore.

It is I in the sun that burns your eyes,
and I in the snow that burdens your limbs.

Your dust speckled glass is but a window
to my earth devoured soul and an ode
to all things come to pass, *including you.*

CAITLIN ELLIS

THE BECOMING

There's a method to my madness-
a solace in decay,
as I fabricate my darkest nights
into my brightest days.

Acknowledgements

The love and gratitude I hold for you, dear reader, is so immense that words fall short. Thank you. Thank you thank you thank you.

To Hunter, for your unwavering support and belief in my ability to see this through. You have loved me through it all.

To Mum and Dad, for encouraging me to always do my best and follow my passions wherever they lead me.

To Emily, for encouraging me to continue posting my work online, even when it felt silly, and to Rachael, for always hyping up my work.

To Rebecca, for turning a project that existed only in the realm of my imagination and making it tangible. You are magic.

To my friends, whose words of encouragement fuelled me in moments of doubt. You all know who you are.

To my English teachers and school librarians for igniting my passion for words.

And finally, to young me, for being brave enough to dream —

Look what we created!

About the Author

Caitlin Ellis is a poet born and raised on Whadjuk Noongar Country (Perth, Western Australia). Her lifelong fascination with the written word has culminated in her passion for poetry and the freedom it allows to subvert traditional literary conventions.

Caitlin's work examines the mundane and the morbid, candidly dissecting concepts of identity, growth, trauma, and transformation with an implacable focus on highlighting that which is curious and beautiful.

Worm Food and Bone Sand is her debut collection.

www.ingramcontent.com/pod-product-compliance
Lightning Source LLC
Chambersburg PA
CBHW020331010526
44107CB00054B/2070